Real Estate Investing for Beginners

The ultimate guide to building a real estate empire with little to no money down

Cory Miles

Table of Contents

Introduction

Thank you for purchasing this book. If you are looking to engage in the real estate world, this is the book for you. You will learn how to make money, and make your money work for you. Enjoy and best of luck.

Chapter 1
About Real Estate

It seems that you are interested in this fast-paced world. However, before you begin, you have to know exactly what real estate investing is, and what all goes into the process. You really have to be sure that you are prepared for this specific industry, because if you are not properly prepared, then you might need to spend a little more time getting ready. This is an industry that can make you rich, but it can also cause some serious financial drain if you are not ready for the whole ordeal.

This book is here to help you as you embark on the adventure of real estate investing. When you try to go out into the world, you feel like you are alone most of the time. This book will help you feel less alone and misguided by giving you the information that you need to get through each day with more and more progress. When you are trying to start your journey into the world of real estate, the beginner level is actually the most difficult. You have so much to learn, and you have to do well the first time especially, because it is the precursor of your potential in the investment.

This industry is a lot different than a lot of other investing platforms. It is not as cutthroat, but it is still a make it or break it kind of deal. It also can take a good chunk of change to start up. It all depends on your area and what kind of deals that you can find. If you know where to look, then you can ensure that you can get the best deals out there, just keep your eyes open.

I know what you are thinking: "You haven't yet got around to telling me what exactly real estate investing is." And you are exactly right. However, I am getting there now, just needed to prepare you so that you know that even though it sounds easy, and it can be easy, it does take time and effort, along with money.

Real estate investing is the process of buying a house for as low of a price as you can get it, fixing it up and adding value to it, and either selling the house for a profit, or renting it out for a steadier income. This book is going to mainly focus on the second option, because it is the best investment strategy out there. When you are renting a property, you become a landlord, and the people who rent from you are known as tenants. You, as the landlord, have a steady income coming in, while your tenants have a nice place to live where they don't have to pay property taxes, or deal with registering a deed.

This is different from the other ways of investing because no other investment platform allows you to earn a steady income, and make as much profit as you can with renting. If you are smart with your money, you can make almost a seventy-five percent return on your investment over a period of time. However, investing in real estate does often take longer to build up to where you make it past breaking even. With other investments, it may take some time to see a return, but with real estate investing, it can take a few years. Also, with real estate investing, you do not have to sell your investment to start making money. You can keep your investment and still make money off it. That is the greatest thing about this platform. Then, when you are tired of being the one responsible for it, and you have made more money than you could have imagined off your investment, you can sell it which could give you even more money than your profit you made on the house renting it did if inflation has occurred in the market. There are so many pros in this industry, that many people often overlook the cons. Let us weigh both shall we?

Pros

There are many pros in this industry. That is what makes it so desirable. These pros could be the reason that you decide you want to invest in real estate, so let's look at them all.

- **Steady**: Most investments are not very steady. Once you get the money, you have to reinvest it to make any more money. Real estate has the ability to make you continual money with minimal reinvestment. You can also get your money almost immediately, rather than having to sit on an investment for months and years on end to make any profit from the investment. Having a steady income can make this more than a hobby, it can make it a wonderful opportunity for your financial gain.

- **Money:** You can make more money in this business than you can in most types of investments, unless you pick a lucky stock. This means that with real estate investing, you can really start to live your life the way you dreamed once the money starts rolling in.

- **More Hands On:** This is only a pro for some, but it is still a pro. You can be active in your investment, and you call all the shots. This means that if you have a problem with your investment not making money, you can find out why and fix it right away.

- **Safer:** This industry is a lot safer than most investment markets, because you don't have to worry about a sudden market crash. There are always going to be people who need a place to live, and are not able to buy a house for whatever reason, or they do not want to buy a house just yet. So, there are always going to be someone who needs to rent.

Cons

There are some cons in this industry as well. It is important that you know about them, because you do not want to get blindsided by one. While there are not many cons, they may be the reason you decide you do not want to be a part of this industry, so it is better to know about them before you have already invested your money.

- **Money**: It takes this investment platform longer to build up money than the other ones. You have to have patience with it, and be able to keep money incoming from other sources. The less you have to spend in the beginning, the sooner the actual profit will start rolling in.

- **Not Constant**: The steady income does come at a price. You have to continually make sure that there is a paying person in your property, otherwise the money you have come to depend on halts suddenly. You have to work hard to keep your rentals and your properties continually in use so that you have continual money. This can be a struggle in the current financial market.

- **More Hands On**: This is also a con for some people. There are people out there that don't want to be in control of everything, because then, when something goes wrong, it is on them to fix it. That is the case here. If something breaks and it was part of what you provided upon moving in, you are required to fix or replace it.

These are the cons that you will definitely have to think over when deciding on if you want to join the business of real estate investing. If you can live with the fact that this is not a dream money making ordeal, then you may find that in time you make the money you need and more.

If you are asking yourself the question: "Why should I invest in real estate." You again, have come to the right book to get your answer. This would not be a book for beginners if we did not answer that question, or at least give you a little more clarity, so here are some reasons why you should invest in real estate.

- **Be Your Own Boss:** No one can tell you what to do. You call the shots, and you make the decisions. You can decide what color to paint the walls. You can decide which property you want to buy, and how to price it. You work on your own schedule, and answer to no one but yourself. It is freeing and very enticing to have that sort of freedom.

- **Financial Freedom**: Once you get established, and start making a profit, you will be relieved at the financial freedoms that you find yourself enjoying. This is one of the main reasons to become a real estate investor. Imagine being able to take a vacation with your family, and not have to pinch pennies the entire time. Imagine being able to do what everyone wants, so you don't have to see any disappointed faces. How many times have you gone on a family vacation, and one kid wanted to do something that was just too expensive for you to afford? How much did it kill you to tell that kid it just wasn't in the cards to go? With financial freedom to go do those things, you can take back your life, and you can take back the fun.

- **Beating the Odds**: So many people are skeptics that they make up statistics of failure to justify telling someone it can't be done, and discouraging them, when in reality they are just jealous that they don't have the ability to do so. They don't feel like sticking their neck out, so they miss the chance to succeed, and they think that other people shouldn't try either. Succeed to make them even more jealous, but also succeed to inspire them.

- **Tangible Investments**: If you own stocks in a company, it is less thrilling to drive by the building and say, "I own a half a percent of that building" than it is to drive by your investment properties and say, "I own that." This makes it a lot easier for people to see your success as well, just be sure not to brag too much.

These are just some of the reasons for you to invest. There are many more reasons out there, but some are more specific than others so only the basic ones are listed. Try it for yourself to see why it is such a great idea.

Now that you know what real estate investing is, the pros and cons, and why you should invest, if you are still reading, I assume that you are wanting to continue on your journey. Now we give you the tips and tricks for becoming a success. These tips and tricks will help figure out what it is that you are needing to do, and how to make it big.

Chapter 2
Beginning Your Journey

The tips in this chapter are what you need to know to start out, before you even make your first purchase. These tips will walk you through how to plan a budget and how to look for the perfect house without being blinded by the cosmetics of the house. You will learn how to look past the surface, and how to decide if you have found the right property or if you need to keep moving.

This chapter is essential to your success. If you do not start out on the right foot, it can be all downhill from there. You want to have a solid foundation to build an investment empire in which to free yourself from everyday financial burdens. You have to make sure that you are doing what it takes to ensure success.

Budget

The first thing that you have to make sure that you have sorted out is your budget. This means that you have to know exactly how much money you are going to have to begin with. It is essential that you make sure you know exactly how much money you want to spend before you start looking for a property so you do not run the risk of over spending.

However, you cannot just know how much you have to spend, because budgeting goes way deeper than that. You have to set aside money to do a multitude of things. So even if you got a loan for eighty thousand dollars, you still would not be able to go out and buy an eighty-thousand-dollar house. You must make sure that you have money left over to do other things.

For example, you need money set aside to do any necessary renovations. These may or may not be extensive. If you go and you buy a house for eighty thousand dollars, and you find out it needs new water lines, where are you going to get the money? You have to dig into your pockets even more, and if you don't have the funds at the ready, that halts your money-making process, and that is not a good thing.

You also have to be sure that you are able to cover closing costs, because those will get you every time. What people don't tell you is that you often are the one paying the real estate agents fees and filing for all of the paperwork. It all falls on you. Plus, you also have to pay the down payment for the loan which comes out of your pocket. This means that you have to be prepared and have the money set aside to buy a property.

There aren't just renovations and closing costs that you have to think about. You also have to take in consideration that you have to prepare for property taxes, and the property being empty for a time. Filing fees if you have a lawyer draw up your contracts for renters. There are a lot of little expenses that you have to take into account before you set aside your budget for buying a house. Otherwise you will find yourself running out of money pretty quickly.

If you have an eighty-thousand-dollar loan, you do not really have eighty thousand dollars to spend on a house. The best way to budget is to try to stay around half to three quarters of what you have when you are looking for a house. Though realistically you will not be able to get a loan that big unless you have superb credit, and even if you could, as a first-time rental investor, it is best to stay around forty thousand dollars unless you are in an expensive area.

In some areas, forty thousand dollars is plenty of money to find a good rental property investment. Especially if you live in the mid-west, or in a less populated town. In a more populated town you may have to get a bigger loan. However, we will stick with the mid-west figures for now just so you get a general idea of how to portion up your money.

Say you go to the bank. Your credit is decent, but not stellar, and you don't want to pay more than three hundred a month on your mortgage so that you can still make a profit from your rental. The bank offers you a forty-thousand-dollar loan, with only a five thousand-dollar down payment. You say that is perfect, because all you have to put down on a loan is six thousand and you also wanted money to pay the first month payment on the loan.

So now you are planning on looking for a house. You have to figure out exactly how much you have to spend on said house, and still have some money left over to make changes to it, and prepare it for a rental property. That means that you should try to find a house between twenty and twenty-seven thousand dollars. You may think that you can't find something that affordable, and you won't find a six bedroom perfectly updated five thousand square foot mansion. However, you could find a two to three-bedroom house with a nice yard in a quiet neighborhood. It may need work, but you shouldn't have to put too much work into it to make it a nice place.

So, after that, you should plan to put around six to eight thousand dollars into the place, to make it look nice. It may need less than that, however, if it needs more, you should move on. (Always find out how much you need to renovate before closing). After spending that much you have about four to six thousand dollars on the low end left after all that.

That money is to cover closing costs, the cost of hiring and inspector, and other general necessities for the house that you will need before you rent it out. After you have finished all of that you may have at max a thousand dollars left. You should put this money into an emergency fund for the property. That is what you will need if something happens to the house. (You should add to that money on a regular basis, but that will be discussed more later)

This is how you budget your money well, and make sure that you are not going to over spend on buying a property and be up creek with no paddle. You have to have the finances to get this process moving as quick as you possibly can, because time is money, and in investing, money is everything.

Searching for the Right Property

The first thing that you should remember is that you are not looking for a forever home for yourself. You are looking for an investment property that may see a lot of different people living in it, and will need repaired a lot. So, you do not want to find a high-end house with all the fancy furnishings. You want to find a house that looks nice, but also fits the bill for what you are needing it for.

It is important that you follow the steps in this tip group, because you want to find a house that is not going to be a money pit, otherwise you are going to be really in for it in the long run. You want to find a house that even though it may need a little bit of work, does not need to be completely redone. (Unless you bought it for really cheap, like only a thousand dollars cheap).

The tips in this section will help you find that property, and will show you the buying markets that are out there, and rank them on which is the best for a new investor, and which is not the best for a new investor, but can still turn up a few gold mines.

The tips will also walk you through the buy process, and help you find what to look for when you do the walk-through process to find a good house. You want to be sure you find the right house before you sign on the line and become stuck with your investment no matter how good or bad it may be.

The first thing you have to know though is where to look for a house. This is important because you want to find a good deal, that isn't going to leave you high and dry in the end. Remember some good deals are snakes in disguise, so you want to use caution, and your head when you are looking to buy.

- **Real Estate Agency:** This is by far the safest way to go. You will have someone there to guide you, and their goal is to ensure that you are satisfied, and that you have found the right house for you. They will walk you through finding what you need. However, they don't get paid if they don't sell a house, so there is always more pressure to buy when you are not sure if you are quite ready to buy. This is not really a big deal, as they do not force you to buy, and they truly do want you to find a great house, but you also have to remember, the realtor has to look out for their bottom line as well.

- **Classifieds:** There is nothing better than an old fashioned classified ad when you are looking for something. These are pretty safe, because they pay to put the ad in the paper, and most people would not do so if they didn't think their property was worth it. You often can make your own times to check out a house without having to go through a realtor. This means that if you decide not to buy it, you won't have to deal with any guilt about taking up even more time. With classified ads, you have to be careful though. Sometimes there are people who pay to take an ad out, but the house is not worth it.

- **Online:** This one is kind of fifty-fifty. You can find a gem, or you could find a flop. You have to approach this one with caution, and you have to make sure that you are cautious when going to see a house from someone off the internet. Take a friend or two with you. Never go alone. Not everyone is a psycho out to get you, but there are a few. In fact, any time you are going to look at a property without a realtor, it is always best to go in pairs. There is always safety in numbers.

How to find a house online is the real question. Many people post their houses in Facebook Groups. Do a search of for rent/sale groups in your area, and you should find several. This is a safer way to look for houses, because there are several people that know about the house, and the person who posted it. You can set up the time, and if things don't go as expected, then you can warn others as well. There is also Craigslist. This is known as the seedier version of a classified ad, but there are still good houses on there. Craigslist honestly gets a bad reputation. As long as you use common sense, then you will be fine.

- **Auctions:** These are really useful if you have a good amount of money for remodeling, but you want to get a house really low priced. Housing auctions happen when someone doesn't know how to price a property, or doesn't want to spend a long time getting it sold. Generally, these properties are run down, but you may be able to get a gem if you are lucky. However, be careful, banks often auction off unsold foreclosures that have high property taxes on them. If you are alerted to the property before it goes up for auction, check into the property taxes on it. If not, you are taking a risk, and hopefully you get the house for cheap enough to cover all of the costs of the house.

- **Foreclosures:** These are really desirable in their pricing, but they can be snakes in disguise. Foreclosures are when a bank has taken back a house that somebody quit paying the mortgage on. They often put it back on the market for how much is left on the note. This means if the person paid it off quite a bit, the house could be fairly cheap. This will draw you in, but you have to use caution.

These houses can be snakes in disguise. They often have a lot of back taxes that are owed on them. If the house is not reasonably priced enough to cover the difference, then you should walk away as fast as you can. Because the taxes are what will get you.

Once you have decided how you want to go about finding a house, you can start your search. There are some things that you should keep in mind when searching for a house.

First off, take a look at the neighborhood. Is it a safe one? Not many people want to live in a neighborhood that is known for drug or gang activity, so make sure that the property you are looking at is in a nicer neighborhood. In a school zone is ideal, because those are the most desirable houses for families with children who are established enough to afford a house in that area. This means that you are almost guaranteed to have people in your property fairly quickly. Check the rating of the school. The higher the rating, the higher you can price the rent.

Also, you have to learn the average rent prices of the area. You want to stay within the confines of comparable house rent prices, because if you are too high, people will be turned off from your property. If you can keep within the confines of the general rent, and still make a profit, then the property is good to go, however, if you cannot, then you should probably look elsewhere.

You have to look at the house itself as well. Is it in decent condition, does it look like it needs a lot of repairs, will it be costly? This doesn't mean the ugly color of paint on the wall. This means does it look like it has evidence of leaks, infestations, other issues. The best way to figure this out is to have the property inspected. You should save an inspection for the property you are really wanting to buy, though, because they can get costly. For the first walk through, just use your own eyes, and see if you can spot anything that could be a problem later on.

Look into the back taxes, and how much they cost. Also check into see how much it would be for the utilities monthly. If they are high, it could be an indication that there is a problem somewhere that needs to be addressed immediately. If the taxes and utilities are high, it may be a good idea to just go on to a different property. Because you do not want to be stuck with a property that is going to sit empty or be a money drain.

If the property you are looking at passes all the tests, then you can go on to making an offer, and hopefully closing the deal on it. There are a few tips for going to make an offer, so as to ensure that you have a good shot at getting the house.

Rules for Finding a House

- **Don't look for a home. Look for a house.**

  The truth is, you are not looking for something that you could see yourself living in. You are looking for something to make a profit. A lot of people pass up a good investment opportunity because they "can't see themselves in the house, and wouldn't want to market it." However, you could make the house better with just a little work. You are not looking for a move in ready house that suits you, you are looking for a house you can make a decent profit off of.

- **Don't let your emotions control you.**

  Your emotions can get in the way of your logical mind when it comes to a purchase. Perhaps you have found the perfect house, but you won't get a lot of profit. Maybe you found a house that seems like a steal, but has more problems than it is worth. If you let your emotions get in the way, you can seriously cause an issue with your bottom line. You must keep your emotions out of business, and that is what this is. No matter how quaint or perfect a house is, if it is not good for profit, you have to walk away. No matter how good a deal may seem, if you find it is not worth it, don't forge on with the deal. It may seem simple but emotions are tricky in the simplest of places.

- **Don't be afraid of auctions.**

Too many people want to buy outright. They do not want to go to an auction and sit and bid on properties. There are a lot of stigmas about auction properties being duds anyways, when a lot of times, you can get a property for cheap, and even after paying any back taxes, you are still way under budget. For people who want to rent out houses, it doesn't really matter, but for flippers like you, an auction can be a gold mine.

- **Ugly is money**

This is a phrase that you should take to heart. A house may look ugly, but if the structure is sound, and everything is to code, you will find that you can make a great profit with an ugly house. All it takes is a little paint and updating, and the house you bought for under market value goes up in value at least one margin. This is flipping at its finest.

- **Don't Settle.**

There are so many options out there. Don't settle for the first deal you can find. Pick out several options and then narrow it down from there. You have to find what is best for you and your pocket book. Too many people get the itch that they have to start flipping immediately, so they take the first cheap house that they can find without doing any research. Take your time, consider every option carefully. Eventually you can make more hasty decisions after you have established a profit base, and have more knowledge in the field. For now, especially on your first house purchase, you have to be careful.

- *Negotiate, But Be Reasonable:* It is always okay to offer a little less than what the seller is asking, but you have to use common sense. No one wants to be low balled when they are trying to sell something, so don't offer ten thousand dollars on a twenty-thousand-dollar house. Eighteen or nineteen is about as low as you should go, depending on how firm they are on the price.

- *Don't Jump:* A lot of people are too scared to push the envelope when it comes to the negotiation process, so they take the first counter offer that they get from the sellers. However, you often can talk them down closer to your number than their original number if you show you are willing to come up a bit. However, people are scared to anger the seller and lose their chance at getting the house altogether. There is a key to knowing when to jump and when to hold out for more.

It all has to do with the timing. You have to pay attention to how quickly they counter. If they counter pretty quickly, then you have a good chance at getting it closer to your number. However, if they respond really slowly with a counter, then if you are able to afford what they are counting reasonably, then it would be best to take it. Also, pay attention to how much they come down from their price to see how much you need to come up. If they come down a little, you should come up a little. If they come down a lot, be willing to go up some more to find a compromise.

- *Don't Make Threats:* A lot of movies and television shows portray a person threatening to walk over a minute difference in their numbers when buying a house, and the sellers contact them with an offer they can't refuse. This is not how it works in the real world. More often than not, a seller will let you walk so they have a better chance at selling the house closer to their desired number. The seller does not have to play chase, and most will not even attempt to pursue you when they know that they have the upper hand.

- *Ask to Split Closing:* In your offer, you should always ask for the seller to split closing costs, so they do not all fall on you. Closing costs can get expensive, after paying the realtor, and filing all the paperwork with the right departments. Most sellers are prepared to help with closing, and have an escrow set aside to do so. If you are lucky, some sellers will cover closing if you settle on a number that is closer to their asking price.

What to Do When You Find a House

So, you think you have found the perfect house? Well, there are still a lot of things to do before you close the deal. The only exception is with an auction house. You have to do some of these things before the auction. So, this section will be broken down into two parts. A regular sale/foreclosure sale, and auction houses.

Regular Sales

When you find a house that is being sold, there are a few steps you have to take. Whether the house is being sold through an agency, direct through the seller, or a foreclosure, you have to do some background checks on the house. Everything that you need to know is public knowledge, so you don't have to worry about paying an arm and a leg when you are looking into these things. The first thing that you have to look into is the neighborhood. How does the neighborhood look? Is it clean and well kept? If so, that is a good mark for the house. If not, that is a mark against it. Two marks against a house, and you should move on. The look of a neighborhood is very important when it comes to profit. People are more likely to buy a house in a neighborhood that is clean and nice looking. If neighbors have broken down cars all over their yards, and grass that is really tall, or houses that are just in shambles, then you will have a harder time selling the house.

The next thing that you have to look into is the crime rate in the neighborhood. This is one of those things that is super important to look into. If the crime rate is too high, even if everything else seems okay, then you should probably move on to a different area. No one wants to live in a neighborhood where there are going to be sirens every other day. They also don't want to live in fear that they are going to get robbed every time they turn around.

School districts are pretty important as well. Make sure that the location is in a school district that has a good rating. The better the rating, the more desirable the location. You will draw in young families who want their kids to have a good education, and the better the school district, the more you can sell the house for. Which is great if you find one that needs work, causing it to be really cheap, and you fix it up well. Profit will swim your way with haste.

Back taxes. The nastiest word in this business. To properly sell a house, it is best to pay up the back taxes on it. A lot of houses don't have back taxes, but especially in the case of a foreclosure, you can never be too sure. You always have to do a check. It is a simple thing to do. Just call the local city office, and they will tell you if there are taxes owed on the property, and how much they total up to.

Once you have looked into all of these things, you should get the property inspected. This does not happen until you are talking deals, but it should happen before you close and shake on anything. An inspection can alert you to anything that is wrong with the property that may not be visible to an untrained eye.

Auction Houses

When you first start out, it is best to go to a visible auction. These are auctions where you are alerted to the property ahead of time, and have a chance to check it out. With these auctions, pretty much everything is the same, except you may not be able to get it inspected, unless you have a friend that is an inspector with you when they allow you to walk through the property.

With a blind auction, you do not get to see the property, most times you do not even get the address until the auction. This is where having a phone with data is important. As soon as you get the address, pull it up on Google maps, so that you can check out the house, and the neighborhood. It will give you an idea as to if the house is worth it or not. Pull up any specs on the property that you can. You have to be quick so that you can start bidding. It is best to go to these auctions when you are more advanced at the process.

Avoiding a Mishap

There is no secret that buying a house can be tricky. What seems like a great property can really cause you a lot of headache. You have to be aware of the warning signs when you are looking into a property.

- **#1 Pushy Seller**

  The first warning sign of a problem is a pushy seller. Generally, these sellers will get agitated when you ask any questions about the property, and they would prefer you to just buy the house without doing any research. They may be insulted that you want to check into back taxes, or have an inspection on the house. If you run into a pushy seller, it is best to turn tail and run.

- **#2 Ramshackle Neighborhood**

As stated above, a ramshackle neighborhood is already a mark against the property. However, it goes deeper than just aesthetic. If a property resides in one of these neighborhoods, generally the property itself will have problems, because there will be no competition to make the property look nice, and to keep up with the maintenance.

- **#3 Weak Handshake/No Handshake**

It is a fact that a weak handshake or a lack of handshake should set off alarm bells. Handshakes help you judge whether a person is trustworthy or not. If they don't shake your hand, or barely touch you when they do, then the seller probably has something to hide. This may be followed by lack of eye contact as well. Body language is the best warning sign there is.

If you watch for the signs of a bad property, you should be able to avoid the problems that come with a bad property.

Those are the tips to successfully negotiating the buying of your first investment property. Once you have obtained the property, it is time to move on to renovations.

Chapter 3
Renovating and Getting Move in Ready

Once you have bought your first investment property, you then have to renovate and get the property ready for people to move in. This means that you are going to have to do some planning. You always have to have a plan after you buy a house to make a time frame for getting the house on the market and rented out. To make the plan you must first establish what needs done to the house, and then decide if you are doing the renovations yourself. (Not recommended if you have no experience unless only cosmetic things need done.) You also have to decide what can stay and what can go in the house. That allows for a time difference as well.

Once you have a plan set in place, it is time to start the renovations. There are some tips for how to go about renovating, and how to save money in order to ensure that you can have a nice emergency fund set aside.

Renovating

When renovating your house, there are a few things that you should know. These tips will help you save money, while still delivering a quality rental in the end. Just because you saved money, does not mean you are "cheap", it means that you are smart, so long as you made sure to spend money where it was needed. These tips will not only help you save money, but will also help you distinguish between saving money and being cheap.

- *If it Works:* If it works, leave it! If you do not need to replace something, then you should not. You are not making a dream home for yourself, you are making a house for others to live in. It needs to be functional, and look decent. That means if the house came with appliances, but they are not the newest ones, leave them. If the tenants want to use their own, then they can. If the cabinets are in good condition, leave them. Try giving them a coat of paint if you don't like the way they look.

- *Clean:* Sometimes, a house is in such good condition, that all it needs is a good cleaning. More than the seller did. Polish the wood, shine the glass, make it look shiny and new. If it has carpet that is fairly new, just have it deep cleaned. (Unless previous owners had pets. Then it has to be replaced.) You would be surprised at how nice things look with just a little finessing and elbow grease. Of course, most first-time investments need a little bit of work, but if you are lucky enough to find one that just needs cleaned, then you are best to leave it at that, and save your renovation money for an emergency fund.

- *Alternative materials:* These are great! Linoleums have come a long way than the green and white ugly kitchen floors of the seventies. Now almost every textile has a laminate copy. This is a great thing, because linoleum is affordable, and if it gets damaged, it does not cost an arm and a leg to get fixed. It is also pretty durable, so it can withstand a lot. There are a lot of other alternative materials out there as well, that look like high end products, without the high-end price tag. This means that you can get a good product affordable.

- **Reuse:** If you want to replace something, try to use it elsewhere in the house. Like say you want to put a better bathtub in the master bathroom to really separate it as the master bath, use the current working tub in the guest bathroom if it only has a shower. (As long as there is space). Anything that you can reuse, then you should try your best to put it to use. Waste costs money. And if you lose money in waste, that is literally money in the trash. In this industry, money is the goal, and the more you lose, the farther you are in your goal.

- **Garage sales:** Not everything bought from a garage sale is cheap. There are often a lot of quality items that are found in garage sales if you are looking hard enough. A lot of people are only selling the stuff because they don't need it anymore. Especially in country club areas. And a lot of stuff the country club people just give away, because they don't need it anymore and were just going to throw it away anyway. Just be careful to be sure not to invite pest infestations in your own home. Checking the item over with a flashlight should prove to show you if it is clean or not.

- **Only DIY Where You Can:** It is the general consensus that if you do everything yourself. This is not necessarily the case. If you know how to do something, then by all means, save yourself the money. But only if you really know how to do it, and have successfully done it before. Otherwise you could be in for a heap of trouble. Knowing how to do something does not refer to watching a video online, and then saying that you are an expert. If you are going to do it that way, take out a thousand dollars, and throw it in the trash right now. Because that is essentially what you are doing when you do this. Except in cosmetic cases where anyone can do those, if you are trying to do everything DIY and you have no experience at all, then you are running a high risk of making things worse, rather than better. An expert may cost more upfront, but in the long run will save you money, because with a repair man, it will last a long time and truly fix the problem, not cause a bigger problem later.

However, if you do know how to do something, do it. Don't spend money on something you can save it on. Your goal is to be able to make a profit as soon as you possibly can, and the more you spend on startup, the longer it will take to make that money back. If you know how to fix a busted pipe, don't hire a plumber. If you know how to change an outlet, and fix faulty wiring, don't hire an electrician. When you hire someone, they charge you for as much as they can charge you without being a scam artist. They charge you for having to travel to the location, for the parts they use, for their time, and for their labor. This is a very important thing to remember, because a lot of people want their rentals to be professionally worked over, and then they wonder why it cost so much to get the work done. It is because these people are trying to run a business, and you don't make any money if you are only making what you put in. You have to do what you can to keep the costs low, and be able to still deliver a quality house to your potential renters.

- *Friends are Essential:* If you have a few good buddies, enlist in their help to get the job done. It is cheaper to pay your friends than it is to pay professionals, and you will save money in the long run, because even though you are paying other people, you will have the house ready to rent out sooner, which means less time that you are paying on the mortgage yourself, and the sooner you can start making a profit.

These are some tips to help you through the renovation process. Avoid big box stores. They deliver below quality products for a high price. Liquidation outlets, and other low-priced stores are the best way to go. You can get quality products for a low price. Liquidation outlets buy overstock from companies, or things that were going to just be thrown out due to damaged packaging, despite the fact the product was still in good condition. This means savings for you, because they can pass those low prices down. The product is often some pretty good stuff as well. So, you don't have to worry about your rental being a basic "cheap" looking place.

Speaking of cheap, there is a huge difference between affordable and cheap. Cheap is when you don't fix something, because it is "not that bad" and you don't want to spend the money on it. And then when it completely breaks after a tenant moves in, you try to put that on the tenant to pay. Cheap is also buying the lowest quality things that you can find because they are the absolute cheapest without caring how it will hold up. Being cheap actually gets rather expensive. However, buying affordable products does not make you cheap, as long as the product is still of decent quality. If you make sure that everything that needs fixed is fixed properly, and you still put quality products in your property, no matter the low price, you are not cheap.

You want your property to be comfortable, and inviting. However, if you put really expensive products into your rental, and you spend a lot of money on renovations, you will never make money, because you will have to constantly fix or replace them. Tenants live under the pretense that if it breaks, they are not responsible, because by law, it is the landlord's responsibility to take care of the property, and replace something that breaks. Unless it is in the contract otherwise, you have to replace anything that is damaged. Since the tenants do not feel responsible for the property, they are more likely to not treat it with care than they would be if they were the owner of the house. This is why you charge a deposit on move in, to ensure that when they move out, you can fix any damage, but if you have high end products in your home, the deposit is not going to cover an entire overhaul. However, if you have affordable products in your home, it is a lot less expensive to replace the materials that are damaged. You want to be able to save as much money as you can to put in an emergency fund so that you are not digging into your profits if something goes wrong with something on the property, such as a sewer line rupture, or something of that effect. Or even little things, like a robber busting the window or the door jam. You want to be able to make the needed repairs without having to worry where the money comes from. However, we will talk more about emergency funds and how to create one later on.

Now it is time to move on to staging and getting the property ready to show. These tips are important for making your property look like a potential home, rather than just a house.

Staging

This is something that a lot of rental property owners try to skip, because they feel that it is too expensive to do, and they do not want to shell out that type of cash. However, staging does not have to be expensive, and you need to stage your home, otherwise you are going to have a property that sits empty for longer than you wish. Houses sell thirty percent faster with even just basic staging.

Staging is important, because it shows the potential tenants what the house is really like, and shows them with a reference if they will be able to fit in the house reasonably. A lot of houses look roomy when they are empty, however, most people know this, and so they shrink it in their mind to the point where they won't think they will fit well. With staging, they can get an accurate representation of the true size of the house.

Staging does not have to be elaborate, and you don't have to have perfect matching furniture, and a full sectional couch in the living room, along with a thousand-dollar bedroom set in the master bedroom, you just have to show people what the room size is like. There are a few affordable options for staging a home, and they all depend on if you are furnishing the house, or if you are just staging it to show it.

If you are going to stage the house just to show it, then you are in luck. This is the most affordable thing to do. Because there is such a thing as cardboard furniture. This is a great resource, because it is very low cost to do, and pretty easy to make as well. Cardboard furniture is exactly what it implies. Furniture made from cardboard.

To create it, all you need is a lot of cardboard boxes, tape, hot glue, and scissors. You can get cardboard for free or pretty cheap at most big box stores and supermarkets. They often have pre-flattened bales of it, which is really useful for your project, and if they aren't free, you can generally buy a large bundle that weighs over fifty pounds for a couple dollars. This should be plenty of cardboard for a standard sized rental. There are a thousand tutorials online for making various cardboard furniture projects. You can buy a big bundle of hot glue at your local hobby store along with a hot glue gun for under ten dollars. For the tape, general paper-like scotch tape. There is actual cardboard tape that is sold by packing companies, and it looks like it is made from a brown paper bag, however this is a little more expensive, and completely unnecessary, because it will be covered anyway. I'm certain you know where to buy scissors if you don't already have some. Make sure to get strong ones, as cardboard is hard to cut through and rough on standard scissors.

When you are covering this furniture, make sure not to use something water based, especially if painting. You do not want the cardboard to warp. You can cover it in fabric, stapling it down, or you can wall paper it. There are a lot of options out there for making it look like real furniture.

The upside to cardboard furniture is that it is easy to move, and if made right, it is durable, however, if you are just making it to stage, and you don't make it strong, it is easily damaged when someone goes to sit down, so make sure to tell people viewing the house that the furniture is simply prop furniture, and not to lean on it unless you took the extra time to make it strong and durable.

If you are staging a house, and leaving the furniture, then you need something that is a little more real than cardboard furniture. However, it does not have to be high end. Free furniture advertised in ads online works quite well as long as it is in good condition, and has been thoroughly checked for bedbugs. Often, you can go in the alley by the dumpsters behind furniture stores and you will find brand new beds and chairs just thrown out because they got a little stain on them or a tiny tear in the upholstery. These are the best, because they are in almost brand-new condition aside from a few little cosmetic issues that are easily fixed, and maybe being a little dirty from being in the alley. Garage sales, and moving sales are also a great way to get furniture and appliances for a low price. You can generally get good quality things from these sales, and they won't break the bank. You don't have to have matching furniture, but if you can find matching sets for a good price, then by all means snatch it up, because the more cohesive it looks, the more desirable it is. However, chances are, if the tenants need a furnished property, the will not mind if the couch is a different color than the armchair, if they don't clash.

If you can't find free furniture, or any garage sales or moving sales, then look online and at liquidation outlets. Online you can buy second hand furniture for cheap, and there are groups on Facebook that are literally called online garage sales. They are especially useful in the winter months, when garage sale season is pretty much over. You can still find furniture and appliances for a good price. However, if you can't find any there, then you should look at liquidation outlets.

Liquidation outlets are going to be a little pricier, because you are getting brand new items for a lower price, but not second-hand low. However, it is still less expensive than big box stores. You can buy some good furniture that maybe isn't name brand for a good price and set up your property elsewhere.

If you can't find any of these, maybe it is best to not furnish your home and just stick with cardboard staging. You don't want to break the bank for furniture that you will probably have to replace when your tenants move out.

When furnishing the house, however, always give the tenants the option to bring their own furniture, and provide them a place to store what is already in there if they need to. A lot of people prefer their own furniture, unless they do not have any furniture of their own. These people are few and far between unless you live in a college town, and then it is a bunch of young adults house sharing, and most of them don't have their own furniture, so they look for pre-furnished housing. However, in a general area, the only people that need a furnished house is someone who was homeless and recently got a job and needs a place to live, people who lost their home to disaster, and people escaping abusive relationships. There are a few exceptions, but those are the general reasons.

Always keep the place clean and shined up. If you have a showing that day, go in a half hour early to dust and sweep up and run a bit of furniture polish over the woods in the house. This just gives the house a brighter feel, and will make it more appealing to people who are walking through, because everyone wants to move into a nice clean house, and when you show it to them when it is shiny, they will instantly be more attracted to it. Keeping everything gleaming will get your property rented out faster than you would think.

Those are the tips to getting your house ready to show. This is the most rigorous process, once you put it on the market it gets a little easier, however, there are still a few tips about being a good landlord and picking the right tenants.

Chapter 4
Picking the Right Tenants

There are a few tips for picking the right tenants and making sure that you will not get played in the end. There is a plethora of good tenants out there, but there are always a few apples in the bunch. Checking the applicants is a great way to make sure that you are not at risk of getting the short end of the stick.

There are a few tips to checking the applicants and where to raise some red flags, and where to proceed as normal. Remember, you have the right to refuse a rental to anyone, just make sure that it is for legitimate reasons, and not discrimination against any race, religion, age, height, weight, or disability. Some states even require you to allow anyone of any marital status live in your property, some do not.

You also have the right to deny any pets, unless they are registered as a service animal. Then you cannot deny the animal, as it is not considered a pet. You are allowed to require proof of the animal being registered, however, you are not allowed to ask for what disability the animal assists the person with. However, the only animals that are able to be registered right now are dogs and cats. Horses are able to be registered as therapy animals, however you are not required to allow a horse to live in your property, as they are only eligible to be registered if the person lives in the proper area. You don't have to worry about someone having a monkey or pygmy pig and saying that you have to allow the animal because it is a service animal. Any documentation that they have is forged, and these people can be reported for fraud.

When you are looking for tenants, make sure to charge a small application fee. This fee will weed out the people who just want to move in for the bare minimum, and who may not have a large enough income to afford your property. It will also be to cover the cost of background and credit checks. You should always run these to decide if your tenant is the right fit for your property. You should also do reference checks on your tenant as well, because you need to ensure that they have a good renting history, and are not searching for a new rental due to eviction.

It is important that you meet the people who want to move into your property as well. Always do a walk through with them, and get a look at them, and see if they put in the effort to look nice to meet you. You want someone that is going to take care of your property, and if they are unkempt, they probably will not be able to do so. Dressing nice doesn't mean a three-piece suit, it just means something a little better than holy, stained clothes. If they look clean, and their clothes look well taken care of, that gives you the impression that they are good at taking care of things. However, if their appearance is the only red flag that they have, then you should not hold that against them. They might have just got off work, and didn't have time to change, because they did not want to waste your time. You cannot be snobby about their appearance, however, if they didn't want to pay the application fee, and their background, credit, and reference checks come back with negative results, and they look unkempt, then by all means say no.

After you run all the credit checks, and find the right tenant, it is time for you to write a contract and start being a landlord. There are some tips for that as well, as you want to be sure that you keep the tenant in the property for as long as possible.

Chapter 5
Becoming a Landlord

Once you have a tenant ready to move into the property, you have to draw up a contract. While you are in the process of looking for a tenant, before you even make a decision, you should do some research of laws in your area involving what you are allowed to put in a contract for leasing, and what you are not. Here are a few federal ones that are mandated across the United States. If you are in a different country, you may have different laws.

You cannot put in a contract anything that requires your tenant to be okay with you entering the property any time that you want. You have to allow them their privacy, and give reasonable notice when you want to enter the property. You are not allowed to do "inspections" on the property to check up on how the tenants are treating it. This violates their property. You are able to enter the property to make repairs and make sure that the house does not need anything. When the tenant moves in, that becomes their personal living space, and they are technically buying the house for the months that they are in it.

You cannot place signs on the property without prior written approval from the family. This includes for sale signs and political signs. However, you can put them on the other side of the sidewalk, which is technically city property. Once you cross the sidewalk, that is the tenant's space, and you have to respect that.

You can't force a tenant to pay rent on an unlivable establishment. If something important breaks, and you do not fix it, the establishment is deemed damaged. If that something is a water line or a floor, or a roof, the establishment is deemed unlivable. If this happens, and you do nothing to fix it, the tenant can choose to terminate the contract and move out with no obligation to pay you the rent that they owe on the rest of the contract, as you voided it by not ensuring that the property was livable.

These are some federal laws that are in effect, however, it is in your best interest to do some research on local laws, because laws differ from state to state. The more research you do, the better it will be if you do get stuck with a tenant that refuses to pay, and you have to take the person to court. If there is an infraction in your contract, that could skew the odds more into the tenant's favor. You want to protect both your rights, and the tenant's rights, but mainly your rights. So be vigilant in your quest to making a contract up.

If you do not feel confident in your contract writing abilities, you can use a site like LegalZoom which will help you write up a contract. For a small fee, it will walk you through the process, and help you find the laws for your area on the leasing sector. Or you can have an actual lawyer draw one up, though this can get pricy, it is the most likely to be ironclad.

Also, always get your contracts notarized. This means that you sign in front of a notary, and you have a truly legal piece of paper. It generally costs less than five dollars, and it is recognized by more courts as a valid contract than one that is unnotarized.

Being a Good Landlord

You want to be a good land lord. This means that you have to be an all-in person. You have to be hands on, and keep an open line of communication with the tenants. However, you must also respect their privacy. Check in with them on occasion to make sure that everything is going good, but don't be overbearing.

Also, if something breaks, be prompt to fix it or have it fixed. Don't leave your tenants without a dryer if you were the one who supplied the dryer in the first place. Don't make a family go without heat in the middle of winter, just because you don't want to get out in the cold or pay to hire a serviceman to do it for you. You must do the unpleasant work, along with collecting the rent.

Be understanding, yet firm. If your tenant is running a little late on the rent because their car needs to be fixed, then be understanding. However, if they are late every month, put your foot down, and demand they become more current with their rent. Hard times happen, but you can't let that drain you of your profit. A one-time deal is okay, but not if it happens every month.

Have an emergency fund. If you do not have an emergency fund, how are you going to fix things when they break? If you do not have any money at the time, you are going to get bit in the rear end. You can have your tenants fix it and take it off their rent, but that could be a lot of rent lost if it is a big thing. Otherwise you may find yourself in a pickle if you don't get it fixed and your tenant has to move because of it. It is always best to take a portion of the money you get from the rent each month and put into an emergency fund to ensure that you will have money to make necessary repairs.

Chapter 6
Do's and Don't

This is a business where you want to be on top. You want to make a good impression to attract people to you. Not only do you want to attract buyers when you go to sell a house, you also want to attract sellers when you go to buy a house. There are some sure-fire ways to attract people to you when you want to do anything with your flipping process.

How to Attract Sellers

The first rule is to remember that you are not entitled to getting anything off the asking price. In today's age, so many people go in feeling like they deserve for someone to take their lower offer just because they put the offer in, and this instantly turns a seller off. Another tactic that people have geared towards is going in with everything that is wrong with a property, and acting like they are doing the seller a favor for even being interested in it. This is not the way to go. You will not get any leverage this way, and you should remember that it is in your best interest to keep the seller happy.

However, if you play your cards right, you will be able to get the seller to be more open to your offers, rather than sticking with their original asking price, and not wanting to budge. This is something that you just have to use a little finesse to obtain.

When you go in to make a deal, do your best to get a face to face meeting with the seller. By asking for a sit-down discussion, the seller can be sure that you are truly interested in the property rather than wasting their time. This will already cause them to be more inclined to want to do business with you. When you go into the meeting, make sure to start with a firm handshake and solid eye contact. This will help you establish a connection with the seller, and you will also be able to gauge how trustworthy they are as well.

Start out by asking them what they have put into the house, and if they have any emotional investment to the property. Seeming interested in why they are selling it will help the seller feel like you are not just there to buy the property, you are there to buy their property. It makes a big difference, even though there is only one word changed in between the sentences.

Tell them all the things you like about the house. Emphasize on them so that the seller knows that you truly are interested. Then go into what needs to be worked on with the property. You could say "I really love these parts (insert positives here), but I do have a few concerns. (insert negatives here)" This way you are not completely dogging the property, and the seller will be more open towards negotiating on the bad parts.

Seal the deal with a solid handshake once you reach a comfortable price for both you and the seller. This will help close the deal and ensure that they will not take a higher offer before you close.

Attracting Buyers

When you go to sell your property, you want to sell it fast. This means that you want to attract buyers. There are several ways that you can do this, but this section will focus on the three main ways that you can do so.

Hang Signs

Of course, you want a for sale sign on the front lawn. Make sure that the sign is big enough to attract the attention of people who are driving by. If you are not going through a real estate agent, then you can hang your own sign. Make it decorative and inviting, but keep in mind people are only going to see it for a few seconds tops, so make the writing big and keep it short. Your sign may be what draws people to your property.

Host an Open House

This was briefed upon in a previous chapter, but it should be stressed that an open house shows that you have nothing to hide about the property, and that you want people to come in and enjoy it. To really attract people, offer refreshments, and be there the entire time to answer any questions anyone may have. An open house will really get people attracted to your openness and will help you when it comes to selling your property.

Host Meetings with Potential Buyers

When someone is interested in your property, offer to meet them face to face and take them on an in-depth tour of the property. This will show the potential buyer that they matter, and show them that you are not all about the money. Establishing a connection will make people want to buy your house, probably pretty close to asking price.

As with any subject there are always dos and don'ts. There are things that you absolutely should do, and things that you absolutely should not do. This chapter will talk about those things through every stage of the process. If you feel like the information in this book is getting a little overwhelming, don't worry. In the next chapter, it will all be broken down into a step by step guide to success. But for now, here is a little more information to pad your success rate. The more you know, the better, especially in this business.

Buying a Property

Do: Make sure you do your research. Check out everything that you need to know about the neighborhood, the school district, and the crime rates. Also check into back taxes. Doing your research will help save you a lot of money in the long run.

Don't: Forge ahead with the negotiation process not knowing what is in store for you. You have to have some idea of what you are getting into in order to make sure that you are getting a good deal and not walking into a money pit. Money pits are the worst, and if your first property is one, you will lose all encouragement to continue.

Do: Get the property inspected before you make any sort of solid deal on the house. The house may look great on the surface, but even the most beautiful house can have a lot of dark secrets hidden among its nooks and crannies. An inspector can tell you if it is worth it to continue on with the negotiation process.

Don't: Jump in with both feet. You always want to make sure that you are making a sound investment. You cannot do that if you get too emotionally invested in a property to the point where you refuse to note that there are flaws that could cost you a lot of money. Make sure that you are making a sound investment, and do not forgo the inspection.

Do: Look for a property that is good for your bottom line. You want to look for a property that takes the least amount of money to gain the most. Or even one that takes a lot of work but is so inexpensive that it is worth it. You want to find a property that helps you grow financially.

Don't: Look for a property that suits you and your family. You are not looking for a second home for you and your family, you are looking for something that brings in an extra income for you and your family. Thinking in the way of what suits you can cause you to miss out on a lot of great opportunities.

Working on a House

Do: Find some great materials that are easy on your budget. There are a lot of alternative materials out there that can make the place look great, and be even better for your profit line. You want to go for these materials, because again, you are not going to be the one living in it. You want the house to have some appeal, but you do not want it to be completely to your taste, and you do not want to break the bank on renovations.

Don't: Put a lot of expensive, high end products in your property. Unless you are selling a house in Beverly Hills, you are not going to get enough money to cover the costs of these products from your property. This can severely hurt your bottom line, and the bottom line is what you are wanting to protect. It is better to go with materials that look nice but are not super expensive for the property you are flipping.

Do: Find creative ways to save money where you can on quality products. There are a lot places that you can go to find great deals on stuff. These places are places such as liquidation outlets, and garage sales. You can also find alternative materials, and repurpose some materials.

Don't: Cut corners to cut costs. This will be noted in an inspection and can hurt your bottom line. People will not want to pay your asking price if you do not do quality work when renovating a house. You have to do quality work and put in quality product, even if it means paying full price for something.

Do: Add quaint and interesting touches to the house. A pop of color with paint is really an eye attractor, and paint can be easily changed. A feature wall can draw the eye to an area of the house that should be most noted, and can also be changed fairly easily if someone chooses to do so.

Don't: Fashion the whole place in your style. What works for you might not work for other people. It is best to keep most things neutral, and add just a splash of style to draw people's attention to things. While you want the property to stand out, not everyone has the same taste as you.

Do: Stage the home with a good amount of style. Add pops of color with pillows and fabrics. Curtains are a great thing to use as well. People should be able to see themselves in a space, and they should be able to have a good idea of the best possible furniture arrangements.

Don't: Show an empty, barren house. No one can truly imagine themselves in a space that looks like it was made for prison inmates. It is a common misconception that showing an empty house makes the rooms look bigger, when in reality, it just makes the house look barren and boring.

Do: Find creative ways to stage your property for a little amount of money. Use your creativity and create furniture, or repurpose old furniture that you can find for cheap. Find good deals at thrift stores and garage sales. Scour the internet for affordable furniture.

Don't: Buy expensive brand-new furniture to stage a house. Because once you sell the house, you are going to have to store that furniture until the next time you sell a house, and that costs money. Anything that costs you money involving properties is a hit to your profit margin. So, go for cheap furniture, it is not going to be there long, and it won't hurt to let it go with the house.

Selling a House

Do: Put it up for sale as soon as you have finished remodeling or staging. Time is money, and money is important in this game. The sooner you have it posted for sale, the better chance you have of selling it quickly, and that is a good thing.

Don't: Put it up for sale before the work is finished. This can cause you to miss out on a lot of opportunities because people will want to see the property right away, and if it is not ready to be shown, they would rather move on than wait for it to be finished.

Do: Host an open house, be present, bring refreshments. Get to know people, and answer any questions they may have about the house. Give them a number to contact you with any questions.

Don't: Leave someone in charge of your open house who does not know anything about the house. It is best to be there personally so that you can make sure that all questions are answered correctly, and that people are getting a connection with you.

Do: Meet potential buyers face to face. Allow room for negotiation as well. Everyone wants to feel like a winner, and if you both can walk away with a little bit of a win, then you will both feel good.

Don't: Do everything over the phone, and don't be a stickler or a pushover. You must be lenient on price, but not too lenient, because that is your income you are dealing with. You also can't be so firm on the price that negotiating is not possible. You will not sell fast that way.

Chapter 7
Extra Tips for Maximizing Profit

Once you have found a suitable property, and have had it inspected, you can make an offer on the property. It is always pertinent to keep in mind that the seller has to make money too, and if you try to offer too low, you could close them off to any further offers from you.

Yet you still need to make a profit as well. The best way to go is to find a good middle ground, that is towards the lower end of your budget so you have some negotiation room, but not too low so that you can still continue the negotiation process on the property. A lot of times a seller will not accept the first offer that you throw at them, so you have to find a good middle ground that allows you negotiating room without going over budget.

When making a negotiation, especially your first, you should have someone there that knows your top dollar, and can help you stay within the means of that budget. They will tell you when you should walk away, because sometimes it is hard to see for yourself when you need to just cut your losses and walk from the deal and continue your search. Often times, when a person gets into the negotiation, they become committed to getting the property no matter what, and that can cause budget problems that can really hurt your profit.

You should always have the property inspected before you go into the negotiation process. That way you can take the results of the inspection into the negotiation, and use that as leverage to try to get the number down more into your zone. If there is anything wrong with the house that could be a potential problem, then you can use that to try to either get the seller to cover all of the closing costs, or cut down the price considerably. Either one saves you money. If the seller is already covering closing costs, then you will find that it will be easier to get the ball in your court, because the longer it takes to sell, the more the closing costs are. You want to make sure that you are paying attention to the other party's returns. When they get to where they are not budging much on the price, maybe by a hundred dollars, you have pretty much reached the negotiation limit. It is at that point you can either make one final offer close to their counter, or take their counter if it is reasonable.

Negotiations are often tricky, but there are a few things that you should keep in mind when you head into one. These are not necessarily rules, more like guidelines that are important to follow. You want to follow these guidelines as close as you possible can for most negotiations, because this will help you set a solid negotiation foundation.

- **#1 Firm Handshake**

  Of course, this only applies when you are meeting the seller in person. However, a firm handshake sets the tone for the entire negotiation, and can help the seller be more friendly and open towards your offers. They say first impressions are important, and they truly are, so it is best to start with your best foot, or in this case hand, forward

- ## #2 Never Low ball

Low ball offers are the bane of a seller's existence. A good rule of thumb is to never offer below two thirds of the asking price. Anything under two thirds is an insulting offer, unless you have proof that the house is only worth that much.

- ## #3 Don't Seem Too Eager

Take some time to think over each counter offer that the seller sends back to you. Figure out a good way to counter back, or ponder taking the offer. Never seem like you are willing to do anything to buy the house, because that leaves you open to being taken for granted. You want to appear as if you are just buying a property and you couldn't care less if you had to walk from the deal. This will make the seller more interested in appeasing you, because they will see that you will not take anything less than a reasonable offer.

Above all, just use common sense when it comes to the negotiation portion of making a deal. There are so many things that you can do when you are negotiating with a seller that will cause them to want help you out, and most of them have to deal with being a good poker player. If you have a good bluff, then you can win a negotiation.

Maximizing Profit

Money, the thing that makes the world go round. It is quite the fickle thing. Misuse it once, and you could have problems that stem from that misuse for a long time. However, play your cards right, and you will find that money is not a problem for you. It all depends on how you play the game of life.

This business is all about the money. The bottom line. The profit. You can't keep this business going if you don't have the profit. You have to have money to buy and flip each house that you are looking into, so each property has to bring in a good amount of profit. There are several ways that you can do this, and each way has its own pros and cons.

- **#1 Stay away from bank loans**

  Bank loans seem to be the hardest thing to gain a profit from. While they may help you get a better property because you have access to more money, often times, the interest rates kill any profit you can manage to get, plus having to pay the loan back even if you haven't sold the house yet can cause a lot of problems. The best thing to do is to save up your own money until you get a sizable amount and then you can move on to buying a property to flip. Or you can ask a friend to go in with you and split the profits down the middle. If you find a good enough deal, you will both end up with a good amount of profit, and you can take the profit you made and find another property.

- **#2 Do the work yourself**

A lot of the stuff that needs done to a property, you can probably do yourself, unless the property needs an entire overhaul. Cosmetic things such as changing faucets and painting walls, laying floors and hanging cabinets do not take a degree in carpentry to do. All you need is a little elbow grease and maybe a few YouTube videos.

Doing a lot of the work yourself can help you tremendously when it comes to saving money. You do not have to pay labor costs along with the cost of the product because you are doing all of the labor. While it is not a good idea to do electrical, plumbing, or roofing if you do not have previous knowledge, everything else such as framing walls, doing drywall, and all the updating is fair game. You can save thousands by cutting out the labor costs. These labor costs can help you out towards pocketing profit, because the less money you put into the house, the better the profit when you sell it.

- **#3 Remember the neighborhood**

A lot of people only focus on the house when they go to do the renovations. They try to make the house look as nice as they possibly can to attract more people, and while making the house look nice is a good thing, there is such a thing as too nice. If you have a house that sticks out in the neighborhood as too fancy, you will bring the value down tremendously, rather than raising it up. This is because the curb appeal goes down when your house looks too nice, because it sticks out like a sore thumb. Add a fresh coat of paint and fix the broken porch, but don't make the house look like it belongs in a homes and gardens magazine if the rest of the neighborhood doesn't match.

- **#4 Staging is important**

Something that is seen as unimportant can help sell your home for a higher price. It does not have to be expensive, a lot of times you can make cardboard furniture to help stage the room, and just add decorative pillows and curtains to go with it.

People want to see themselves in a house, and if they can't see themselves in a house very well, it makes them less apt to give a higher offer. However, if they can see just how well the space works, then they can begin to see their stuff in each room, which will make the house more desirable. You want to make sure that people desire the house and want to offer you what you deserve for the property.

Those are some of the ways that you can maximize your profit when you go to sell your first property, however there is a massive way that you can save money and make a better profit that has nothing to do with the property at all. It is known as a budget.

Budgeting

Admit it, you kind of cringed at the word. Budgets are seen as a constriction of free will when it comes to money. However, they are necessary in this business to keep you from going overboard with your money. They are necessary in life really. You have to have a budget to ensure that you are making the right moves when it comes to buying and flipping a house. The better you are with a budget, the better your profit margin will be.

There are three things that you should remember when it comes to budgeting. These three things will help you become proficient at creating and maintaining a budget to ensure the maximum amount of profits available. These are mini rules that you can follow to help you out as you learn the ropes of real estate budgeting

- **#1 Split the Budget**

  It is not enough to have a budget of money that you cannot go over. If you do that, you run the risk of spending too much in one area, and not having enough for something else, which will often leave you having to go over the amount you intended to for the whole deal.

  Instead, you should split your budget up into groups, and allocate a certain amount of the funds to each group. One group can be buying a property, another group could be for renovations, and another smaller group could be for staging the house. Or you could have the third section as emergency funds. You can split it up into as many groups as you would like, however you would like. You should just make sure that you split it up.

- **#2 Know Your Accountability**

If you are not that responsible with money, you should have someone help hold you accountable through the entire process to ensure that you do not go over your budget. It may make you feel silly having someone looking over your shoulder ensuring that you do not spend too much, but it will help hold you accountable until you learn to do that yourself.

You should not be ashamed that you have a hard time managing money. A lot of people have the same problem. The only difference is that you must learn to manage money quickly so that you can keep yourself from making a flub when it comes to your profit margin. You must know your level of accountability though, otherwise you will not be able to know if you are spending too much. Listen to the input of others around you, and pay attention to how you are in a store. If you buy unnecessary items that you really don't need, then chances are you do not have enough control on your money to go at this alone.

- **#3 Keep Track of Everything**

Every purchase you make should be logged and accounted for. Even if you just bought a box of nails, or a pack of batteries for your flashlights. If you are using it for the house, mark it down. This will help you see where all the money is going so that you can make some changes if need be. If you find that you are spending too much on screws and nails, look at the sizes of boxes you are buying, and maybe just go with the bigger boxes to save money in the long run.

By keeping track of every single purchase you make from the time you buy the house (that purchase should be logged too) to the time you sell it, you will be able to get an accurate representation of how much you made in profit, and how much you could have made if you had done things a little differently. You will be able to learn from your mistakes, and do better the next time around.

Making a budget is a great way to maximize your profit, because you can be sure not to spend too much on any aspect of the flipping process.

Conclusion

Thank you again for your purchase. Hopefully you learned everything that you needed to know from reading this book. If you liked this book, please leave an honest review on Amazon.